A Buyer's guide to buying land

Questions you need to ask. Answers you need to know.

By

Steve Hooper

Copyright 1995

Revise 2016

Bruce County Public Library
1243 Mackenzie Rd.
Port Elgin ON N0H 2C6

Introduction   page 1.

Let's get started   page 2.

What's next?   page 4.

Going forward   page 6.

Get the facts   page 15.

Corner markers   page 18.

Water   page 20.

Sewer/septic   page 23.

Zoning and land use   page 25.

Environmental concerns   page 27.

Electricity   page 33.

Grading   page 33.

Hire an engineer?   Page 34.

Easements   page 35.

Flood Plain   page 35.

Fault line   page 36.

Permits   page 36.

Other questions   page 37.

About the author   page

INTRODUCTION

Hi Everyone, I have been specialized in selling land for 32 years now. I've sold land to small contractors to build infill housing tracts and to big gun developers to build large housing tracts.

I've sold land to sub-dividers who buy land and split it up and sell off the lots.

I've sold commercial land where they built a tilt up concrete building for a store front.

The contractors, developers, sub-dividers and commercial builders know there way around land sales. Most know what to look out for and what questions to ask.

The sale I like the most is to the families. The individuals who want to buy some land to build their own home. It's a place to call their own and raise a family.

I've helped many, many families buy land for this reason, and as their families have grown I've helped their kids buy homes of their own.

There are a lot of things to be concerned with when you make the decision to build a house. A lot of buyers are un-aware of what they need to ask and where to find the answers.

The BUYER'S GUIDE brings up a lot of the concerns and issues that most buyers don't think about.

It takes a lot of planning to build a house and make sure all the bases are covered. It's harder than it looks, but it is very rewarding to know you put your heart and soul into building the house of your dreams.

The BUYER'S GUIDE goes over the purchase agreement. Also there are many questions covered that might pertain to your situation on purchasing land.

The feasibility study you will do is crucial to making sure your costs are in line and you're not getting over your head.

Everyone has different reasons for buying land. Some for investment some buy land for their young children so it will grow in value for their future. Some buy to develop.

They subdivide and sell off the lots or build homes on them for others. Many buy to build their dream home. Many feel that this is the way they want to go. They want the feeling of building their very own custom home.

Whatever your reasons are, I'm sure they are important to you. My advice is simply, get professional advice first. Get your ducks lined up first.

Talk to your tax person, see your lawyer, and talk with a loan officer to see about land and construction loans and what they require in terms of down payment and overall loan cost and monthly payments. Make sure you qualify before you write an offer. Make sure this is what you want to do.

It is also very important to get a good real estate agent. One that knows land and one that can help you in being sure you get the property that will allow you to do what you want to on it.

I have been a real estate agent for 32 years now, and I've specialized in land sales. There are definitely some very important questions to ask about a property before you buy. That is the reason for this BUYER'S GUIDE.

It is important for a buyer to know what important questions to ask and how to get them answered. In answering these questions, it also might help in deciding if the reason you are buying is the right reason.

LET'S GET STARTED

Fewer than five percent of land sales are by investors who are buying the land for the future or to hold for their family. That means that ninety five percent are buying to build. About thirty percent of those are for commercial buildings, residential apartments, and home development. That leaves sixty five percent of the land sales going to folks buying to build their dream home.

This BUYERS GUIDE will help on any of these purchases and make you aware of what you need and what you should watch out for.

You can call on the "For sale by owners" and real estate companies searching for the right piece for you family. This will take time. You will need a lot of information to make the right decision. If you believe you have found the right lot, but the owner has limited information for you, then this BUYERS GUIDE will help you point out the way to getting the right answers you need.

My advice, just seek out a good real estate agent who knows land sales. Here's why, you will soon realize once you start looking for some property, you will learn that about ninety percent of the land for sale is through a real estate company.

If every real estate company in town ran an ad on just the land they have for sale and they all ran those on the same day, I believe you'd have a classified section that is as large as a phone book.

You will probably only see less than one percent of the listed land for sale in the newspaper. Most real estate companies only run ads on the attention getters, the ones that will make the phone ring.

Nowadays you can find anything online. Most real estate companies have all their land listings on their webpage and in the multiple listing service.

There are still several real estate companies that run ads in the local newspaper.

When you find a professional to work with, you need to let him or her do the

2.

work for you. Tell the agent exactly what type of property you want. Tell them the area you would like, the size of the lot, the topography, and all the details and requirements you would like.

The agent will put this information into their computer system and come up with only the ones that fit the bill of what you are looking for. This is very important to you because it can save you so much valuable time and energy.

I had a client who was only interested in finding land to start a growing nursery on. Some land that had the kind of soil he could grow a special kind of tree in. This property had to have a certain type of climate throughout the year.

I found it for him because I knew where to look to find the right information for him. A good agent who sells land knows the area and can be invaluable to you in your search.

Make a commitment to work with the agent and be loyal. An agent will spend hours upon hours searching for those pieces of land that are just right. They deserve your loyalty.

Most people don't realize that an agent has access to every listed property in the multiple listing service. There is no need to go looking all over town when your agent has access to all available properties.

If you see a sign on a property and you want more information on it, just call your agent, they can get you the information with a lot less hassle. Be loyal. Trust them, they will work hard for you.

The choice will be yours. Find the property on your own or work with an agent. The game plan is still the same. Now we look at the plan as if you have already found a piece of land you like. What's next?

3.

WHAT'S NEXT?

Let's pick out a lot as an example. This parcel is located outside of town in a nice rural community. You like the land and the view. It has some nice trees on it and a seasonal stream.

This lot looks like the one you have been looking for. You know there are a lot of questions to be asked before you are sure this is the right lot for you.

I want to make a strong suggestion to you right now!

WRITE UP AN OFFER ON IT FIRST!!

You see many buyers don't understand how an offer works. Most buyers believe that when you write up an offer that they are locked in and there is no way out.

TOTALLY WRONG!

Why do I believe you should write an offer to the seller at this stage?

Because in your offer you are not only asking the seller to accept your price and terms, but you are also asking in your offer to have time to complete a feasibility study to your satisfaction.

The feasibility study will give you the time you need to answer all the questions you feel are necessary to be sure that this is the right property. The type of property you are buying will determine how much time you will need to do the study.

4.

In most cases, when the escrow is going to be 30 to 45 days, the time frame is between 14 to 20 days. If you are buying commercial or multifamily land, it might require up to 30, 60, or 90 days to do the study.

If the seller accepts your offer on the price and terms, or if he counters them to something that is acceptable to you, then you still have that time frame in place to examine the property.

What have you done up to this point?

You have tied up the property for the balance of the feasibility study. You must state in your offer that by the end of your time frame, you will approve or dis-approve your findings in writing. If you dis-approve the study within the time frame, you will receive your earnest money deposit back and go look for another lot.

If you go past the time frame that was agreed upon in your offer, you could lose your deposit. If you approve the study and you are satisfied with the land, you approve it in writing and get ready to close escrow!

So you ask why can't I just get these questions answered before I write up an offer?

Well you can, but you can also lose the property. You can spend two weeks getting all these questions answered only to have someone else write up an acceptable offer to the seller. Then you would have wasted all that time. Plus, if you spend all that time on getting the correct answers and you don't agree based on price and terms, you have lost again. So consider which way you wish to go and then go forward.

5.

GOING FORWARD.

Depending on what part of the world you are in, an offer to purchase vacant land will be different from one area to another. Overall they contain the same basic features that will get your terms and conditions presented to the seller in the manner you request.

The thing you have to remember when writing up an offer is to ask the seller to provide certain items and information when you write an offer.

Let's go over the offer, which ties into the questions. The first page deals with the financing. What you are doing is asking the seller to also accept your offer to examine the property. Unless you are completely happy with what you find out about the property, you don't have to close.

You also ask the seller to provide you with certain things which we will go over later on.

I'll say that the asking price on the lot we are buying is $50,000.00. You will have to research to see if this is a good price or not. Comparable sales for property in this area can be acquired from your real estate agent or from a local title company.

So after checking the comps, you decide that the price is fair. Next try finding out how long the property has been on the market. If it has been on the market a long time then the seller is more likely to look seriously at a lower offer.

You should ask the seller or their agent up front before you write the offer and ask if there is anything owed on the property?

If the seller has a loan on it, can it be assumed?

Does he need to pay it off when he sells the property?

6.

The answers to these questions will determine how or if you will write an offer and at what price. The worst situation might be that the seller has to come up with the cash to pay off their existing loan.

This just means that you have to have the cash or get a loan to buy this property so the seller can pay off the loan. If the seller has an assumable loan, you may be able to take over their loan in making your deal.

If the property is free and clear, you are in much better shape. It has always been much harder to sell a piece of land that has a loan on it.

You will need to ask if the seller will carry back a note and first trust deed on the property?

If you are working with an agent they will have a purchase contract available to write up an offer. You will need to show proof of funds to the seller to show that if all goes well you have the means to close the escrow.

If you are getting a land loan, you will need a pre-qualification letter from the lender showing you are qualified for the loan. You will also need to show where your cash down payment is coming from.

Usually this is a bank statement.

If you are paying all cash, then show proof you have all the cash required to close.

When you start writing up your offer remember to,

PLEASE READ EACH LINE CAREFULLY

7.

On the first page we want to state who is making the offer. If you are married, then make sure your spouse's name is on the offer and they sign it.

The earnest money deposit you put in is a strong selling point. The deposit tells the seller how serious you are about buying their property. Try 1, 2 or 3% of your asking price.

Next put down the price you wish to offer. This price is based on some of the research you did earlier. The address and assessor's parcel number comes next.

You might have a loan contingency, unless you are paying cash.

Do you wish to increase the deposit during escrow?

This will depend on if you are able to put down a strong deposit up front or if you can put 1% up front and another 1% in 14 to 21 days, usually after approval of your feasibility study.

Show the balance on the down payment you are putting down on the property.

State the terms you would like. This is where you would ask the seller to carry back a note and trust deed, or ask to assume a current loan. Or state that you are getting a bank loan, or paying cash.

However you decide to purchase, when you add up all the numbers, the deposit, the down payment, the additional terms, they should equal your asking price.

If the seller agrees to carry back a first trust deed and you are planning to build within a year or two, you might want to ask the seller if they will subordinate to your construction loan?

8.

Subordination is when a person holding a first trust deed on a piece of property is asked to move to a second position and allow a new first trust deed to be placed on the property.

Usually this new first trust deed will be from a bank or mortgage company for the purpose of a construction loan. Some people have a real hard time with this. They are taking a risk. You would ask the seller to subordinate now in the offer even if you were not planning on building for several years. If the seller agrees then the subordination should be drawn up by an attorney. If they do not agree, then you will have to close with enough money to pay off their loan.If the seller carries any part of the purchase price an additional financing disclosure needs to be filled out and read over carefully. This form details the terms of the loan the seller will carry and if it will have certain conditions, such as,

A due on sale clause, also,

notification to the seller if you are not making your payments on the other loan.

Next is allocation of cost. This details who is paying for what.

Usually escrow is paid for by both buyer and seller equally. Other items will vary depending on the area and circumstances. The seller usually pays for the preliminary title report and title insurance. It's much easier when you are making an offer that you want the seller to accept, to leave the door open to them deciding who the title and escrow companies will be.

You can put down "any reliable" on your offer. That will allow the seller to choose the companies they prefer to work with, making it easier to accept.

Next tell the seller how long you would like the escrow time frame to be,

30 days?   45days?   90 days?

9.

If you got your down payment money and the seller is carrying a first trust deed, then 30 days should work for you. It depends on your situation. The time required will depend on how much time you feel you will need to do a feasibility study. Once the study has been completed you could close soon after.

Title insurance is usually paid for by the seller, but that could very in your area. During escrow you will receive a preliminary title report on the property. This report will tell you if there are any liens, encumbrances, restrictions or easements on the property to be concerned with. Easements and restriction usually stay with the property. Verify with the title officer what liens and encumbrances will stay with the property after the close of escrow.

Important!! ASK FOR A COLOR CODED EASEMENT MAP.

This will help you see any access issues you may have to deal with.

You will get to review this report and will need to approve it in writing. Go over it carefully and ask the escrow officer or the title officer any questions or anything on the report you do not understand.

In your offer ask for a copy of any CC&R's, which is covenant, conditions and restrictions. These will tell you what you are allowed to do or not to do on the property.

Proration's, is a section that deals with how items will be paid. Usually this is property taxes, bonds, assessments, interest, rents, dues, etc. Most of this is just fill in the blanks as to what your request are. Usually the seller pays everything up current until the day it closes escrow then the buyer assumes it after that.

ALWAYS REMEMBER TO READ THE CONTRACT OVER CAREFULLY!

FEASIBILITY STUDY

This study is very important to you. It says that you will do a feasibility study on the property within so many days after the acceptance. This is one of your safety nets. This time window allows you to ask the questions you feel are important to ask about the property.

If I do a 30 day escrow, I usually ask for 15 to 17 days to complete the study. At the end of the time stated you have to make some kind of commitment. If you are unhappy, you disapprove the findings of your study, also in writing, and cancel the escrow. You must do this within the set time frame or risk the loss of your deposit.

Another way to go is if you find something that you are unhappy with, ask the seller if they will take care of it or help you solve the problem. This can work.

NHD

Next, ask the seller to provide you with a Natural Hazard Disclosure (NHD). This is where the seller, or a company of his choice, provides you with flood and geological hazard disclosures.

Then ask the seller to either disclose within so many days if they are aware of any flood, fire, or geological hazards that affect the property?

If the seller has an agent who is representing them, then this information should be in the disclosures you will receive to review and sign off on.

11.

TIME PERIODS

These are very important to you. There are pre-printed time frames on the offer, but those can be changed. Read them over carefully.

MEDIATION AND ARBITRATION

These are buyer's options to initial or not. If there is a problem between the buyer and the seller that cannot be resolved, and both have agreed to mediate and arbitrate, then they would allow a third party to listen to the problem and allow them to solve the issue.

LIQUIDATED DAMAGES

The earnest money deposit you put up lets the seller know that if you back out of the deal for a non-justified reason, then the seller can keep the deposit. Read it over carefully because both parties have to sign for the release of the deposit, regardless of who it is going to. If there is no agreement, then it goes to mediation, arbitration or court.

LINE ITEM REQUEST

This is a spot in the preprinted offer where you can mark the box or write it in and ask the seller to take care of some items. These are items you would like the seller to pay for and not you, but in some cases, you do.

If the property already has a well, you would ask the seller to provide you with a recent gallon per minute certification and potability test done on the water.

The gallons per minute will determine the productivity of the well. The potability test will tell you if the water is fit to drink.

12.

You should always ask the seller to show you where the corner markers are located at. A surveyor or civil engineer can mark the corners at the seller expense, if the seller does not know their location. This is not always done do to the expense and many buyers purchase without the corners being market. This will be your choice.

If by chance there are improvements on the lot like a septic system, then you would ask the seller to pay to have it pumped and certified before close of escrow. If the seller is aware of where the septic tank lids are located, have them show you or mark their location. No guarantee the seller will do this.

Ask the seller to pay for a percolation test on the property, if one is needed.

No guarantee the seller will do this.

There may be one on file with the county health department. This test determines how fast the water will percolate into the soil and if it passes then the county or city will allow you to install a septic system.

Ask for any repairs to be made on any equipment that may be broken, if any.

Ask for a partial reconveyance if you need one. It is used frequently by developers and sub dividers. It means that when a seller takes back a first trust deed on their property and the buyer subdivides or splits off some lots, then the seller will release free and clear and convey to the buyer one of the lots so that the developer can build on it. The seller agrees to put the balance of his note on the remaining lots. In the agreement, the buyer will pay down an agreed upon amount per lot until the last one is paid off. This allows the developer to build out their development.

13.

SELLER TIME TO RESPOND

Give the seller a time limit as to how long they have to answer your offer. In some offers this has a preprinted amount of time, but usually there is a spot to change it if necessary.

Now go back over your offer and make sure it is complete. Check to make sure all spots were initialed and signatures where required before you submit it to the seller.

14.

GET THE FACTS!!

If your offer was accepted, you are ready to move forward toward your feasibility study. If the property is listed then the listing agent should provide you with some disclosures that may or may not cover some of the questions below.

If the property you are buying was not listed, you can write out your list of question and ask them to provide you with the answers, if they know them.

In order to get the facts about this property you are going to have to dig up the answers yourself by going to the source. Don't rely on the answers from the seller, as they may have changed and they are unaware of them. You need to verify them to be correct.

Ask the right questions and try to get the right answers. This list of questions can be asked to the owner or through your agent or their agent.

Your questions should always be in writing with a request for a written response. Your agent can help guide you in getting the answers you need.

NOTE: The agent can guide you to the source, but it is the buyer's responsibility to get the correct answers in order to go forward on this lot or start looking for another.

It is the agent's responsibility to help and make sure you know where to go to get the correct answer. This BUYER'S GUIDE is written with the intent to make sure you know which road to travel down.

Most buyers are unaware of where to start on finding out if the property is a legal, buildable lot. So if you buy without the help of a good land agent to guide you, it makes It tough.

Now with this BUYER'S GUIDE you will also know where to begin and what works for you.

15.

One of the first thing you did before you started looking for some land was to be pre-qualified for either a land loan or a construction loan. If you are planning on building a house on your new lot, you will need a construction loan after you close escrow.

There are so many things to be concerned with when building a house. The bank or mortgage company should be able to provide you with a list of reputable contractors that they have worked with.

Before you start looking for a property, you should call several contractors on this list and get a ballpark price on how much it will cost you per square foot to build a house with the amount of square footage you require.

If you don't have house plans of your own, you should ask these contractors if they have any you can look over to see if any of these plans might be just what you are looking for.

You want to make sure you're up to date on your construction cost. There are so many things to take into consideration when you build a house.

By talking with an approved contractor, who works will with the lender you are using, they can guide you with some of the expenses you will be concerned about.

How important is this information to me as I look for a lot?

Assume you were pre-qualified for a land and construction loan amount of $150,000.00. The rule of thumb is 1/3 of the total value of your completed house is what you should spend for a finished lot. The lender can help you estimate the cost of construction or guide you to a reliable contractor on their approved list. This is needed regardless of whether you are building a house or buying a manufactured home.

16.

In our example you will find out that it will cost you $95,000.00 to totally complete the construction on your home or manufactured home, including permits. The completed value on your home is $200,000.00.

This will leave you $50,000.00 to $55,000.00 to buy a finished lot

What is a finished lot?

A finished lot is a lot that is ready to build on. It has everything ready to go. It has water, gas, sewer, and electrical available. All you need to do is build the house and hook up to the available services.

If you find a lot that needs a pad, well, or a septic system, or if you have to have electrical brought to your lot, you will have to reduce your buying price by the estimate of these costs, or work these items into your construction cost.

17.

CORNER MARKERS

Does the owner know where the corner markers are?

Sometimes they will know and sometimes they haven't a clue. Many others have bought without knowing exactly where the corners are.

If not, will they pay for a survey?

You should always ask. A survey can be very expensive. Check prices with a surveyor first, if the seller is not willing to pay.

Usually they are more reasonably price than a civil engineer. Buying a piece of land without a survey will be up to you, but there have been many that have. Obviously the corners will need to be located to set up for any construction.

If the seller does know where the corners are, will they show you where they are?

When you are looking for those corners markers, make sure you see the real mc coy. This means the actual metal pins in the ground. Try to walk off the distance between the pins to make sure they are the correct distance between each one.

If the corners are marked but the seller isn't sure where they are, will they pay to have them marked?

18.

This is much cheaper than a survey. This means that the pins are there and set, but their location is unknown. Once a surveyor finds one or two pins, the others are easy for them to find.

Do the property lines go to the center of the street?

If the seller is unaware of this answer, a parcel map should show you. One will come to you when you are in escrow from the preliminary title report or you can get a map from the title company or your local city or county zoning office.

19.

WATER

Is there water available or does it need a well?

This should be an easy answer from the seller. If there is city water, ask which water district it is in. Just in case this is an estate sale, you can call the local water district and give them the parcel number. They will tell you if this is in their district or some other district.

Does it have a well?

Some properties have capped off wells or wells with pumps that have not been used in many years.

If so, does the owner have written proof as to how many gallons per minute it is producing?

Finding out how many gallons per minutes is important. Check with the county or city building department to ask how many gallons per minutes are required before you are granted a building permit. You can get a copy of the original well drillers report from the city or county records.

Will the owner pay to have the well tested for GPM?

20.

You will need to test this one way or the other. You have nothing to lose by asking the seller to pay. Get several estimates on the cost to test the well before you have it done. You can look on line or the yellow pages under "well drillers" to see if they would test the well for you.

If there is a well, has the water potability ever been tested to assure it is safe to drink?

You can check this when you check for the gallons per minute. I'm sure not an expert on wells, but I know of the two types of water sources. One is an underground river that always flows and bacteria does not build up. The other is an underground pond where the water sits and bacteria can build up. If the water test shows that the water is not drinkable, do not be alarmed. It is possible to treat the water to make it drinkable. Check with your local environmental health department.

Will the seller pay for a potability test?

A potability test can be analyzed by a private laboratory, or check with the local environmental health department. I prefer a private company. They seem to get the job done a lot faster. The health department will not let you build without a satisfactory test. You pay if the seller won't.

If there is city water in the street, does it have a lateral line already into the lot?

21.

Besides asking the seller, verify this by contacting the water company in person. Get something in writing if you can. If there is not one in, ask them how much will one cost?

Is there a water meter in place on the lot?

Verify this at the water company. Check the cost of one if there is not one. Get it in writing.

If there is water in the street, but there is no lateral line to the lot, how much will the water company charge to put a lateral line in and a meter?

The water company is not the only ones who can install this line. Get an estimate from a licensed contractor. Save as much money as you can. Remember you are on a budget.

If there is no city water and a well is needed, where do you find someone who can answer my questions in regards to the cost of a well and the possibilities of finding water on the property?

I recommend you get at least three estimates from reliable well drillers in the area you are buying the lot. Compare cost. Each one will probably recommend different areas on the same lot to drill. The well driller looks for rock formations and different types of foliage to tell if they will have any luck in finding water. They can estimate the average depth of the well in the area, but remember

22.

nothing is for sure when you drill a well. There are no guarantees that I know of except you pay by the foot. You will see that having a well can be cheaper than being in a water district. Five gallons per minute is good, eight to ten is better, fifteen to twenty is great and twenty to fifty is a dream come true. Get as many estimates as you feel you need. Ask for references from each well driller.

You can also hire a water witcher if you want. I used one for several years and he found 10 out of 10 where he said they would be. Check on line to see if there are any in your area and if they have references.

Does this water company have any kind of moratorium which would not allow you to be serviced by their company?

There might be water in the street, but they might not let you use it. Check and verify in writing.

23.

SEWER/SEPTIC

Is there sewer in the street or does the property require a septic system?

Ask the seller. If there is sewer available, then ask what company it is. Check out this information and verify with the company.

If there is sewer in the street, is there a sewer lateral to the lot?

Go down in person to the Sewer Company and check and verify, remember always in writing.

If there is not a sewer lateral, how much will the sewer company charge you to hook up to the sewer system?

Just like the water lateral, you can get estimates from other contractors to find the cheapest price you can. See if there is a separate hookup fee.

Is there a sewer moratorium which would not allow you to be serviced by them?

Ask the sewer company. Check and verify in writing.

If the property needs a septic system, has the property ever had a percolation test done on it?

24.

Sometimes the sellers are not aware if it has or has not been done. To check and verify, contact the local environmental health department and see if they have a record of one done on file.

If the seller has papers stating that one was done on the property, can I get a copy from them for your records and to verify?

Always verify this important information.

If the property has not had a percolation test done on it, would the seller pay for one?

A percolation test is when an engineer digs several holes in the ground and pours water in them to see how fast the water seeps into the ground.

If there is no recorded information on a percolation test, what type of engineer do I need to call to find out how much it will cost me to have a test done?

The environmental health department should be able to give you a list of qualified people who can do the job. Also look on line and in the yellow pages, under "percolation test". Get at least three estimates before you commit.

If I need a septic system, who can I talk to about the cost to install a system?

25.

Look on line or in the yellow pages under "septic systems". Get at least three estimates in writing. The ballpark price to install a septic system is around $4500.00 to $7500.00.

If I need a septic system, is this property big enough to build on based on the city or county requirements?

This is important! You building department along with the local health department might require that you have a backup reserve area for your leach field. If this is so, you will need to make sure you can build the house you want and be able to show the building and health department where your septic layout is and where your backup area will be. Go to the building department and the health department and ask for their help. You don't have to have an engineer draw up any plans during your feasibility study. You just need to make sure the lot is big enough to handle the building and health department's requirements.

ZONING AND LAND USE

What is the zoning and land use designation on the property?

Even if the seller knows this information, you should check and verify in writing with either the city or county planning or zoning department. Ask them if there are any plans to change the general plans for the area. If they are planning to change the general plan in this community, it could affect the zoning and land use of the property you are buying.

What is zoning and land use mean?

Zoning will tell you the immediate zoning on this property and it will list under that zoning all the things you might be able to do on the property. The land use designation lets you know if the property could possibly be split into separate parcels and what might be required to reach this based on the community general plan.

Will this zoning allow me to build the kind of house I want?

You know zonings don't change very often, but it is possible. Remember to ask about the general plan when you are at the planning or zoning department. Also check the C, C & R's (covenants, conditions and restrictions) which might state that certain types of homes are not allowed.

27.

When will I find out if there are any Covenants, Conditions and Restrictions on the property?

During escrow. Ask for a copy of the C, C & R's for you to review and approve. If you don't like what you see, speak up! This might be a reason to walk away from this lot.

Could there be building and animal restrictions in the C, C & R's?

Yes, read them carefully. They are there for a reason. Make sure you can live with them.

If I decide to not build right away and wait a few years, is it possible for the zoning to change?

Yes, check the general plan at either the city or the county zoning department your property is in. They can tell you if they foresee any major changes coming in the future.

Can I put a manufactured home on this property?

Check the C, C and R's to verify what they say. Also check with the local building department on what their requirements are.

28.

Can I put an older mobile home on this property?

The local building department should have requirements on age, shape, and size, also the type of permanent foundation you can use.

Who can I ask about how much it will cost me to move an older mobile home or a manufactured home and set it up on the lot so I can get permanent financing on it?

Look on line or in the yellow pages under " mobile home movers" to start. Also call a contractor to discuss your plans and to give you an estimate on the set up cost. Once your home is on a permanent foundation, you should be able to get permanent financing. Before you go too far with this CHECK WITH THE LENDER. Tell them the age of the home and make sure the lender is willing to work with you on this before you move the mobile home onto the lot.

If I am going to buy a property to land bank and resell it many years from now or subdivide it in the future, what should I be concerned with?

Consider the general plan for the area. Ask is there any plans to change or update the general plan in the next couple of years. Is there any other building projects being built in your area? Which way does the building industry seem to be heading? How far way are the utilities from your property? Does the Land use say it can be split? If not, what would you have to do to change this to allow you to split this property? You have to feel that you are buying in the right location and that the rest of the world is right behind you.

29.

Does the zoning allow me to have horses and other animals?

There are two places to check this, one being the local zoning department, which will tell you what is allowed and how many animals you can have. The second is the C, C and R's (if there are any). The C, C and R's are usually a lot stricter than the local zoning laws. You can be fined for having more animals than allowed.

Can the property be split?

The zoning department will tell you the minimum lot size so you can estimate how many lots you may get. Remember in most cases the city or county planning commission will need to review and approve your lot split. You will need to consider about streets and any other requirements they may have. Slope is another concern to take into consideration. If there is too much slope on the lot, you may be very limited on how many lots you will get based on the city or county's hillside review requirements.

Where can I find out how much a lot split would cost me?

There are two ways I know of and one is a surveyor or an engineer. A surveyor can do a simple lot split and usually cheaper than an engineer. Remember, if you split a lot down to four lots and a remainder lot, this can be done locally at the city or county land use department. If you split to more than five lots, then after it is locally approved, it has to be approved by the state. (Check your local area to see if this is a requirement).The local split takes possibly six to nine months. Add state approval, it could go sixteen to twenty four months or more. Ask for a free estimate on the cost and time from several engineers and surveyors. Also ask the 30.

city or county about the fees required to do a lot split.

Should I be concerned about slope?

Yes, if there is too much slope it might not be buildable. You will need to check with your local building department to check on the slope requirements and the hillside review on what can be done. I would also let a grading contractor go give you their opinion. I have seen some beautiful pads built on a sloping hillside that would make you drool. Don't let a slope scare you away.

31.

ENVIRONMENTAL CONCERNS

Is there or could there be any environmental requirements on this property that would not allow me to build on it?

Yes, check with the health, zoning and planning departments. There could be a conservation easement on the property. If you are splitting the lot, you may be required to do an environmental impact report to show what the impact any construction would have.

Where can I go to answer any environmental requirements I might have to meet before I can build?

Check with the city or county health, zoning or planning departments first. Also an engineer that you might hire could answer your questions.

If there are no environmental requirements on this property at the present time, and after the close of escrow I decide not to build on it for several years, could these requirements change?

Yes, everything changes. If you are planning on building or splitting the lot, do it as soon as you can. You can never be sure when things will change down the road. I had listed a ½ acre parcel for a gentleman, who had bought a one acre parcel to begin with. He split it into two ½ acre parcels and built his house on one of the lots. He was saving the other lot as an investment to sell to go toward his retirement. When we checked with the county, the requirements for a septic tank leach field had changed and now required a backup area in case of a failure. This

32.

meant the lot had to be at a minimum of ¾ of an acre to build on. We had only ½ acre and so it shot down his plans to sell this as an extra lot. He decided to go ahead and sell his house and land together, which gave him a better price, as he was on a full acre, but he would have benefited better had we been able to sell the lot separately. Things change.

ELECTRICITY

Does the property have power available to it?

If you can see a power line close to the property, you are in luck. Ask the local power company what the fee would be to get power over to your lot. Depending on the company, the cost could be little or a lot. Check this during your feasibility study because it could be a deal breaker.

GRADING

Do I need to do any grading done on the property in order to build?

This will depend on the topography of the lot and what type plans you have for your home.

Where can I find a good grading contractor to give me an estimate?

Try on line and in the yellow pages under grading contractors. Ask the grading contractor for references. Get several bids and always in writing.

Is there already a pad on the property?

If you see one you should be concerned. If you can't see one, ask the seller. Overgrown brush could be covering one up.

Does this pad have a permit or is it an illegal pad?

Ask the seller and check with the local building department. You must find out this information.

Is it true that if there is a pad on the property without a permit that the pad will not be considered a buildable pad without some extensive test?

Yes! This can also be very costly. The building department usually charges you double the regular fee and if it is not a compacted building pad then you may have to dig it all up and start all over again. Be very concerned if there is a pad.

HIRING AN ENGINEER?

Should I pay an engineer to do a feasibility study on the property?

It's an average price of about $750.00 to have an engineer do the study for you. Call a few up and ask what their study cost and what it covers. It might be the way you prefer to go.

34.

EASEMENTS

Are there any easements to the property or over the property I should be aware of?

Ask the seller first, but request a plotted color coded easement map from the title company with all the recorded easements on it for you to review and approve. In your offer, if you remember, you ask for so many days to review these items in your preliminary report.

FLOOD PLAIN

Should I be concerned about the property being in a flood plain?

If there is a seasonal stream or river on the property you should. Also be concerned if there is a dried up riverbed or old stream, as they may only see water during a heavy down pour of rain.

How can I check to see if the property is in a flood plain?

If there is water of any kind running through this property, then it has some kind of flood plain to be aware of. The first place to check would be the city or county flood control department.

Is it possible that if this source does not have any information on a flood plain, that the property may still flood in the rainy season?

35.

Absolutely

Who should I ask next about this?

If the flood control department has nothing on a flood plain, it just means they have not done a study on the water flow in that area. An engineer would have to do a study on the property and estimate where the flood plain would be on the lot. This must be done before the building department will allow you to build. You can't build in a flood plain and you wouldn't want to anyway.

FAULT LINES

Should I be concerned about a fault line in the area of the property?

Yes, I am sure you would be upset if you built right on top of one.

Where can I find out about known fault lines in the area?

The city or county zoning department should be able to guide you to a fault line map of known fault lines in the area. Once you see if there is one nearby, you can decide if this is the right property for you.

PERMITS

How do I find out how much the permits fees will be if I decide to buy this property?

36.

Ask the building department. Usually they will post their fees on line. Call them and they will ask you the square footage of your home and give you an estimate of your required fees. Remember, while you are there to ask them about permit fees for well, septic, grading and any others that may be required.

OTHER QUESTIONS

How do I know what the value is on the property?

If you like the lot, compare the lot to the sold lots in the area. Your real estate agent can help you with this. They can provide you with comps or you can get them from the title company.

Should I have a contractor look at the site during the feasibility study?

Sure, if you are planning on building something on the lot in the near future. Your contractor could pick up something he sees that could either save you some money or cost you some money. If you are building right away, your contractor could submit your plans for approval during escrow and get ahead of the game. You can submit plans yourself if you don't have a contractor. Just make sure you have already approved you feasibility study and all looks good for closing. It will cost you money to submit your plans.

If I'm using a contractor and I'm getting a loan from a bank or mortgage company to build my house, should I get a contractor that is approved by the lender?

Yes. This will save you a lot of headaches. If the lender already knows how a contractor works, they're going to feel much more comfortable about making you the loan. You can bet that anyone on their list has a good reputation and gets the job done, usually.

If I am building my own home and I don't want to involve a contractor, can I still get a loan to buy the land?

Depends. The best place to get the loan is from the seller. Make him an offer to carry back eighty to eighty five percent of the sales price. Show him you have a good credit rating and can afford to make the payments. The more cash you put into the pot, the better off you will be and the better your chances that the seller will carry back the loan. You can get a bank loan on the property as long as the property meets the lenders requirements. Check around or ask your agent to help you find a lender with the best rates. They usually require 25% to 50% down on the property.

Can I live in a travel trailer on the property while I am building?

To legally put a travel trailer on the property to live in while you are building, you will need to check with the building department. They could require that you submit plans that are approved. Then they will issue you a permit for the trailer. Usually it is good for one year at which time you will need to show progress on your construction before they will renew you permit. Check the policy on trailers at your local building department. You could get a big fine if you don't have a permit.

38.

What if I am looking at buying a property that does not have city gas available?

Not to worry, you can have propane brought in to take the place of natural gas. Look on line or in the yellow pages under "Propane". Get several bids. Talk to your contractor about propane gas appliances. Once you pick a company to work with, they will bring out a large propane tank to your property and set it up. It can be filled by a company deliver truck when needed.

What if I am looking for some land to park some of my construction and heavy equipment on?

Check with the zoning department first on this because this type of equipment usually requires the property to be in a commercial or industrial zoned area.

As you can see, there are a lot of important questions to answer in buying land. These questions can be asked regardless of what type of property you are looking for. What is important is to make sure that you are going to be able to do what you want to do on the property.

If I could emphasize one key thing before I went out looking for property, it would be to talk with a lender first. It is knowing how much you can borrow and knowing how much cash you will need to make the purchase.

Most buyers are unaware of how much cash may be required to put something like building a home or moving a manufactured home on a lot.

If you are a veteran, you are in luck. VA will finance either new construction or a manufactured home. You can check with your lender for details on the VA requirements.

Your real estate agent may be able to recommend several good lenders who can help you on construction loans, land loans, and a VA loan.

Enclosed is a VACANT LAND FEASIBILITY CHECKLIST that will be helpful when you write up your offer. It shows the seller some of the items you are checking into when you make your purchase. Try to include it with your offer so both parties can sign it.

Now that you have found out how much you can get a loan for and how much cash will be required, go find yourself a property. Go find the land, make an offer, ask the questions, and get the answers you want.

Good Luck!

VACANT LAND FEASIBILITY CHECKLIST

This is a condition of the contract that the buyer has the right to do a feasibility study on the subject property to determine the cost factor in developing and improving the property. If for any reason during the allotted time period the buyer is not satisfied with any part of the findings of the study, the buyer will receive a full refund of their deposit money. The items to be checked by the buyer will consist of;

1. **ZONING:**
   Property zoned to the buyers satisfaction
2. **ENVIRONMENTIAL:**
   Buyer is to check with the County or City Environmental Health Department to satisfy themselves as to any issues from this department.
3. **FLOOD PLAIN:**
   Buyer is to check with the County Flood Control to see if the subject property is in a known flood plain area.
4. **ELECTRICAL:**
   Buyer is to be able to verify the cost to run power to the property.
5. **SEWER:**
   Buyer to verify the cost to hook up or possible septic system required cost factors.
6. **WATER:**
   Access cost to local water company or possibility of a well. Buyer is to verify to their satisfaction regarding cost factor.
7. **ACCESS:**
   Buyer is to assure proper access to the property.
8. **PROPERTY CORNERS:**
   Buyer is to be fully satisfied on property corner locations.
9. **GRADING:**
   Buyer to examine expense or any necessary grading requirements to meet buyers needs.
10. **PERCULATION TEST:**
    If property requires a septic system and a test has not been completed, then the buyer is to have access to the property to complete and satisfy themselves on the results.
11. **PERMIT FEES:**
    Buyer to be fully satisfied with the estimated cost on all fees required from the city, county and state.
12. **CONSTRUCTION COST:**
    Buyer is to satisfy themselves on all estimated construction cost of required structure.

_____ _____ _____ _____

BUYER   DATE   SELLER   DATE

_____ _____ _____ _____

BUYER   DATE   SELLER   DATE

ABOUT THE AUTHOR

Steve Hooper was born in a small town in Kansas. He came to California via the U.S.Navy. He was stationed onboard a ship that was home ported in San Diego. Steve did two tours in Vietnam aboard his ship before he received an HONORABLE discharge in 1973.

California was now his home and in 1984 he acquired his real estate license. His first sale was a small parcel of land in the back country of San Diego.

Over the last 32 years Steve has sold millions of dollars' worth of land. Steve has helped develop and sell subdivisions, and commercial property, and apartments. He has worked with developers, land bankers, contractors, zoning and land use officials and building department officials.

Steve's goal is to help the private individual who has the dream of building their own home. "It's important to get the right answers to make sure that dream can come true."

41.

CPSIA information can be obtained
at www.ICGtesting.com
Printed in the USA
LVOW03s1733300616

494764LV00010B/319/P